CU00806694

HOW THINGS FLY

(Original French title:
Pourquoi ça vole?)

Françoise Balibar and Jean-Pierre Maury

Translated from the French by
Albert V. Carozzi and Marguerite Carozzi

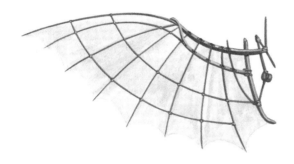

BARRON'S

New York • London • Toronto • Sydney

First English language edition published in 1989 by
Barron's Educational Series, Inc.

© 1987 Hachette/Fondation Diderot-La Nouvelle Encyclopédie, Paris, France.

The title of the French edition is *Pourquoi ça vole?*

All inquiries should be addressed to:
Barron's Educational Series, Inc.
250 Wireless Boulevard
Hauppauge, NY 11788

International Standard Book No. 0-8120-4215-8

Library of Congress Catalog No. 89-6806

Library of Congress Cataloging-in-Publication Data

Balibar, Françoise.
    [Pourqoui ça vole? English]
    How things fly/Françoise Balibar and Jean-Pierre Maury;
translated from the French by Albert V. Carozzi and Marguerite
Carozzi.—1st English language ed.
        p. cm.— (Barron's focus on science)
    Translation of: Pourquoi ça vole?
    Includes index.
    Summary: An introduction to flight of all kinds—by kite, gliders,
planes, birds, etc.
    ISBN 0-8120-4215-8
    1. Flight—Juvenile literature. [1. Flight. 2. Aeronautics.]
    I. Maury, Jean-Pierre. II. Title. III. Series.
TL547.B3513 1989
629.13—dc20   89-6806
                                                        CIP
                                                        AC

PRINTED IN FRANCE

901 9687 987654321

Contents

To Move in Water and in Air

A plane has to move to remain airborne. A helicopter can remain suspended in the air without moving, but the blades of its large propeller must rotate very rapidly! The forces that sustain a plane or a helicopter in the air originate from these movements.

The same forces are produced by movement in water. These are much easier to study because even at very low speed they are quite important. This is why we shall get to know them first.

I t is not possible to run in water that comes up to your waist; indeed, it is even difficult to walk under these conditions! Water pushes backward against the stomach and legs. Water *resists* all the more the faster we move.

Water Resistance

Water resistance pushes us backward against the stomach and legs. Similarly, if one tries to move a well-rounded stick in water, held in a perfectly vertical position, one can feel that resistance pushes the stick in the direction opposite to its intended motion.

Now, instead of a stick, let us try to move in water a wide and thin wooden board, still held vertically. If you are not at the seashore, this experiment can be done in the bathtub or even in a small vat with a smaller board.

Let us move the board like the blade of a knife that would "cut the water." This is quite easy to do: if the board is thin, water resistance is very low.

Now, let us move the board facing straight forward just as the stomach of somebody walking in water: this is much harder to do!

Now, let us move the board,

Water resistance varies both in magnitude and in direction according to the inclination of the board.

still at the same speed, but more or less sidewise. Two things are felt:

— the more the board is facing forward, the greater the resistance.

— the direction of resistance changes with the orientation of the board.

Resistance is always *perpendicular* to the board, that is, directly against it as if it were a nail that one would drive into it.

Therefore, when the board is moved while tilted with respect to the direction of movement, resistance is no longer directed straight backward: it is perpendicular to the board; that is, water resistance pushes both backward and sideways.

Seen from above, the red arrow represents water resistance.

With these observations in mind, it is easy to understand all kinds of movement in water, such as swimming, the use of paddles, oars, sculls, and propellers, and also water skiing and the rudder of boats. Let us begin our discussion with what most resembles a board: the rudder of a boat.

The Rudder of a Boat

When holding the rudder, turned slightly one way or the other, water resistance, which is perpendicular to the rudder, is also sideways. This resistance acts in the most efficient direction to turn the boat, almost without braking it.

However, the boat must move if the rudder is to be of any help: otherwise there is no speed, no water resistance, and no force!

Movement

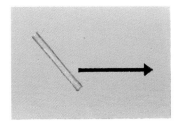

Force

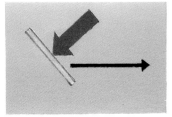

Water Pushes the Swimmer

Why do flippers help in moving the diver forward? Because water resists when the swimmer moves the flippers! While flapping the feet, water resistance on each flipper is always perpendicular to it and hence more or less oriented forward: water pushes the diver forward.

In swimming with breast strokes, although the swimmer has only his or her arms and legs to move, the result is the same as with the board: when he or she joins the two stretched legs, water opposes itself against this joining and pushes the swimmer forward.

The Paddle

This is certainly the oldest way of moving a boat. Whether we are dealing with dugouts carved from a tree trunk as in Africa or Amazonia or light canoes made from bark by the natives of Canada, a paddle suffices to move these boats silently on rivers and lakes.

If we try to do the same, we quickly notice that in order to move straight ahead, the paddle must change sides continu-ously, splashing our feet as we shift it from side to side. Is this really necessary? No, if the paddle is placed in the water slightly sideways, the force of the water is a little sideways, too, and thus compensates for the tendency of the canoe to turn toward the side opposite to that of the paddle.

A Beginner in Rowing

For the beginner, oars appear alive and endowed with an exasperating will of their own. One plunges toward the bottom, the other skims the water, lifting a shower of drops: it seems impossible to move straight ahead! Happy is the beginner whose oar does not jump out from its notch on the rim of the boat.

All this can be easily explained (although we have yet to learn it on the spot despite many misadventures!).

A boat moves forward because water resists the movement of oars. To go straight forward, the movement and the *position* of the two boards must be the same.

Why do oars tend to jump in the air, outside their notches? Water resistance is perpendicu-

Using a paddle correctly is certainly not as easy as it looks!

lar to the oar. If the blade of the oar is not vertical, water pushes it upward or downward. For instance, if it is like this:

it will jump in the air!

To avoid this, it is better to plunge the oar a little bit in the other direction, like this:

Movement

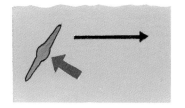

Force

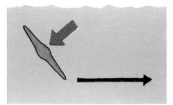

9

This time, the more we pull the oar, the better it becomes lodged in its notch on the rim of the boat.

Scull

Why does the Breton fisherman prefer a scull (an oar, mounted on a fulcrum at the stern, that is moved from side to side) to a pair of oars (see picture p. 5)? Because it occupies much less space outside the boat. This is particularly useful for moving around between other boars, the piers, and the various mooring cables in a harbor. Furthermore, if a boat rides somewhat high above the water and is a little wide, oars for rowing alone would have to be 5 or 6 meters (16.5 or 19.8 feet) long like those of the ancient galleys.

However, the maneuvering of a scull must be learned.

Let us look at the blade of the scull from above as seen by a Breton fisherman. When it moves from left to right in order

that water pushes against it in the direction that propels the boat forward, the blade must be turned one way.

When the scull is moved from right to left, it must be turned the opposite way.

This is why, with a simple movement of the wrist, a fisherman makes the scull swing a quarter of a turn each time he changes the direction of its movement. This seems to be very easy . . . on paper! How-

ever, it takes a while to grasp this movement, which is shaped like a figure eight, which renders the scull really efficient.

As to the propeller in a boat, it works exactly like two (or three) small sculls that always turn in the same direction.

What Happens in the Air?

Now that we have learned about the forces of resistance in water, let us see what happens in the air. Air also resists movement, but much less, and this resistance, called friction, is felt only at great speed. For instance, when racing cyclists want to move very fast (to the finish line, for instance), they lower the head and flatten the body to the bicycle. Of course, they do this partly because this position allows a greater muscular effort. However, they do this above all to decrease their "frontal surface" in order to decrease air friction. The "egg"

To decrease air friction, the smallest possible body surface is exposed.

position of a speed skier has exactly the same purpose.

In regard to water, an explanation is easier for a simpler object shaped like a thin plate, for example, the plastic "feathers" forming the crown of a shuttlecock in badminton.

This shuttlecock leaves the racket with its feathers in front as fast as an ordinary ball. However, soon after, it slows, turns around, and reaches the partner with its feathers behind.

Its slowing down is easy to understand: the crown of feathers increases the surface that the shuttlecock exposes to the air. Air friction is much greater than with a shuttlecock without feathers: the greater the speed, the stronger the friction. However, why does it turn around?

Let us suppose that the shuttlecock moves, feathers first, but slightly sideways (it is actually always a little sideways). If it is in the position shown on the diagram below, air friction on the upper feather is stronger than on the lower feather (this is why one of the red arrows is drawn larger). Why is air fric-

Air friction

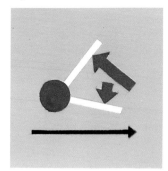

tion stronger on the upper feather?

Let us remember the board in the bathtub. At the same speed, the resistance of water depended largely upon the position of the board: the greater its frontal exposure, the greater the resistance of the water.

The same applies to the shuttlecock. The upper feather on our diagram has a more frontal exposure to air than the lower one and hence it is pushed more by the air and the shuttlecock spins on itself. The upper feather then has an even greater frontal exposure to the air, and the difference between the two frictions is further increased so that the shuttlecock spins even faster on itself. At last it turns around, and this time air friction puts it straight with the ball in front. Now, the two frictions reach the same value.

At this time, if the shuttlecock changed its position only slightly, the difference in friction would put it back to the right position. This is why the shuttlecock has the shape of a horn: air friction forces it to travel with the pointed part in front. It's the ball that meets the racket, not the crown, which would suffer from the impact.

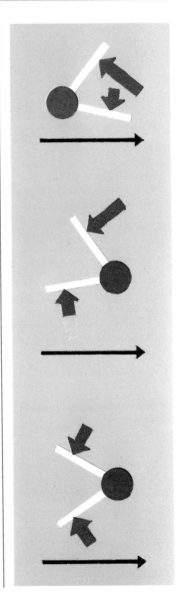

Kites

Kites were invented in China, as was paper and fireworks. Kites have all kinds of shapes and sizes, from small ones looking like butterflies and weighing a few grams that start to fly with a small breeze, to giant ones, as tall as houses, which are operated in Japan by teams of fifty people.

Kites can be made on a rainy day and be flown when good weather returns. Nevertheless, both for their making and handling we should know what is happening: why do kites fly?

To start with what difference is there between the two pictures below? None! However if the rest of the picture is shown, we notice that there is a difference! The effect is exactly the same on the hair and the scarf of the young girl whether she moves fast in calm air or whether she is standing still facing strong winds.

By the way, it is often said with respect to the first picture

Between these two pictures, *there is no difference, however . . .*

14

that the hair has been blown up by the wind of the race. Of course, it was not really wind but air friction during the movement of hair. However, the action of air on hair is the same whether the girl races at 30 kilometers/hour (18.6 miles/hour) in calm conditions or whether winds at 30 kilometers/hour (18.6 miles/hour) blow against the girl while she is standing still.

And if the girl raced 30 kilometers/hour (18.6 miles/hour) facing a wind blowing at 30 kilometers/hour (18.6 miles/hour)? Air friction would be much greater, as much as if she raced 60 kilometer/hour (37.26 miles/hour) with no wind at all! It would be harder for her and this is why, in the second picture, she has stepped down from the bicycle.

Therefore, air friction on an object is the same when the object moves at a certain speed in calm air or when the object is standing still facing winds with such a speed. This is how air friction or drag can be studied on the body of a plane even before adding wings. The plane is placed in a tunnel through which a very fast artificial wind is blowing. Air friction is meas-

ured on the various parts of the plane: it is the same air friction when the plane itself flies at the same speed with respect to air.

A kite, however, does not need artificial wind: regular wind makes it rise in the air—if its string is tightly held. Why?

The String of a Kite

If we let go of the string, the kite falls; it seems strange that it is necessary to pull a kite downward so that it stays up in the air! However, the string is not supposed to pull it down, but to keep it in place and in a good position, that is, in a correctly inclined plane with respect to the wind.

Indeed, for air to push the kite, the latter must first have a certain speed in proportion to its size, weight, and so on. If we let go of the kite, there will be no more relative speed, no more push!

17

Moreover, air usually pushes perpendicularly to the kite. The direction of the push therefore depends upon the orientation of the kite. This orientation in turn is controlled by the way the string is attached to the kite. It is therefore extremely important to attach it correctly: this is the first condition for a well-flying kite.

Most often a "bridle" is used, that is, a piece of string attached to the top and the bottom of the kite that is twice as long as the kite itself. To the bridle is then attached a long string with which the kite is held. The location at which the bridle is attached is called the connection, which is very important because it controls the inclination of the plane.

Force

If the connection is placed too low, the kite's position is too upright. The wind force will be very strong but with a very small upward inclination. If the string does not break and if the person flying the kite has enough strength to hold onto it, the kite nevertheless does not rise very much.

If the connection is placed higher on the bridle, the kite is less upright and the wind force not so strong but directed more upward: the kite is carried better, with less effort on the string, and rises higher.

Bridle

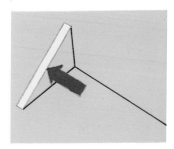

Finally, if the connection is placed too high, the kite is almost horizontal and the wind force is insufficient to fly the kite unless the wind is extraordinarily strong.

This important position of the connection depends upon the shape of the kite, and it can be found only by trial and error. Most often, it is located close to the upper third of the bridle.

The Tail of a Kite

Flat kites made of paper stretched over a light frame must have a tail. This is not only for decoration but also to avoid spinning of the kite around its string and to keep the kite's upper part up and its lower part down. In fact, it is the tail that pulls the point of the kite, not only by its weight but also and above all because of the force of the wind that presses against the tail at the back of the kite. Therefore, the length of the tail and the size and the number of attached paper bows are adjustments that are as important (and easier to make) as the location of the connection. If the tail is too heavy, the kite cannot rise. If it is too light or too short, the kite swings around its string, "skidding" violently to the left, then to the right, then to the left, until it falls to the ground. Why these zigzags? It is too difficult to explain in a few words. But it is very easy to see, and rather easy to correct: the tail must be lengthened, that's all!

How about kites without tails? Many models exist, all of them more complicated than flat kites. They can fly without tails because they have something else to keep the upper part up and the lower part down. For example, box kites are reinforced on their sides by large strips of stretched fabric that prevent them from swinging around themselves and skidding (it is never easy to move a "board" head-on).

Other models have a triangle of fabric replacing the bridle and playing the role of antiskid. They are called keel models because the triangle of fabric resembles the keel of a boat. This device plays the same role as we shall see later when talking about sailboats.

Sometimes, certain flexible kites take on the shape of a keel by themselves.

However, the flat kite has none of these devices to prevent it from gliding sideways and swinging around. What it needs is a tail.

To Adjust a Kite According to the Wind

Depending upon wind velocity, a kite can be adjusted differently. There are two kinds of adjustments: the connection of the bridle and the tail.

If winds are very strong, the connection can be attached higher up to make the kite fly more horizontally, or the tail can be lengthened or thickened to "anchor" the kite firmly in the air.

In contrast, if wind velocity is low, the connection must be lowered to increase wind force or the tail must be shortened to lighten the kite. Since it is rather tricky to change the connection of the bridle, it is often preferable to leave it where it is and simply adjust the tail.

Nevertheless, these adjustments have their limits and there is no such thing as an "all-weather kite." Some kites are very light—and hence fragile—for light breezes; others are heavier, made from a fabric or strong paper for strong winds. Of course, the string, too, is not the same in the two cases.

With a heavy kite, and a strong wind, it is possible to raise small loads along the string. One must invent a system of small sails that carries the load along the string and that retracts at a certain elevation so that the load returns to the ground. Thus aerial pictures can be taken if one is careful that the camera does not fall too fast.

The Wind as Engine

Wind force is used not only to raise kites: for a long time humans have also used it as an engine. It turns mills, either the old windmills for grinding grain or the modern windmills for activating a dynamo to produce electricity.

It is also wind force that pushes sailboats.

This is easy to understand if the wind comes from behind the boat. It is even more astonishing when the wind comes from the side.

Here again, the wind force is necessarily perpendicular to the sail. Should the boat therefore move in the direction of that force? This would occur if the boat were round and had a flat bottom. However, the boat's elongated shape and in particular its keel (a straight board attached to the bottom of the hull) prevent any sideways crablike movement. It is difficult to move a board in water other than in its proper direction (as the blade of a knife).

A well-built sailboat can even "sail to windward, that is, almost against the wind.

Of course, in this case the wind force hitting the sail is less than if the boat sails before the wind: when the sail is perpendicular to the wind, it offers a larger surface. However, what really matters for a boat to move forward is that the wind force is always perpendicular to the sail.

In the case of a boat that is sailing to windward, with the smallest practical angle to the wind, the curvature of the sail under the pressure of the wind

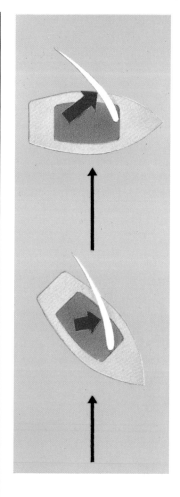

develops aerodynamic behavior comparable to that of an aircraft wing mentioned later.

Sailboat

22

From Dead Leaf to Glider

A glider propelled into the air at a certain speed does not fall to the ground like a stone. Instead it glides sideways, descends very slowly, and flies a long distance before landing.

Real gliders, capable of carrying pilots, are of course complex aircraft. Before talking about them, let us mention a glider that is much simpler, namely a paper glider called a flying wing. To start with, we shall observe the circling of dead leaves.

Why do dead leaves fall in a zigzag? First, it is often the wind that detaches and carries them along in its eddies. Nevertheless, even without wind, a dead leaf does not fall straight to the ground: it descends gliding sideways, most often in a zigzag.

A leaf descends in a zigzag because it is not flat. It is always convex on one side and concave on the other. Air friction immediately turns the convex side forward, and for a falling object, forward means downward. Hence the leaf glides toward the ground sideways with its convex side turned downward.

Air thus has a tendency to

"Flying Wing"

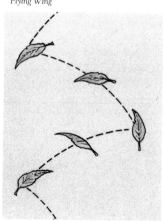

push the leaf's front edge upward and its back edge downward. The leaf thus glides increasingly on its side, and finally it rises, slows down, and stops. At that instant, if the leaf comes for example from the right side, its left edge is raised upward. Therefore, it turns right again, that is, in the direction where it came from. And so on, until it reaches the ground in zigzags.

If a sheet of paper is dropped, something similar happens. However, since the sheet is flexible and flat, it changes its shape and its descent does not show a clear similarity with that of a dead leaf. It must be made rigid and bulging to fall really like a dead leaf. Therefore, if an ordinary sheet of paper is cut down the center and its two middle edges glued one on top of the other, a sort of very flat bag is obtained, a "dead leaf" that falls like one. (see diagrams a and b on p. 27).

The Flying Wing

A flying wing is a "glider" without body and without tail. It glides downward and sideways, sustained by air resistance like a dead leaf but without making a zigzag. Therefore, it must have both a front and a back edge and should be heavier in front than in the back so that it glides in that direction. And of course, it must "bulge" so that air can press on its raised back edge to maintain the whole in a correct position.

A flying wing can be made so that it resembles a dead leaf, but with more precision:

— Fold into four a sheet of ordinary paper such as that used in a typewriter. Cut halfway through the center along the small fold. (figure c).

— Fold into two the half that is uncut.

— Fold this once more into two.

— Flatten the folds well (figure d).

— Place the wing down flat with the fold on top, and glue together the two edges of the slit, making them overlap 1 centimeter (.4 inch) at the edge of the sheet. This is enough to make the wing bulge a little opposite the slit, the side that is therefore its "belly."

The first flying tests can be attempted. Throwing the wing in the right position is enough to give it a little bit of speed. It does not make zigzags like a

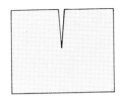

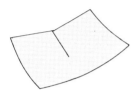

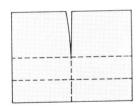

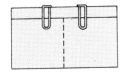

dead leaf, but its movement is not perfect as yet. Generally, its defects are:

— It leans sideways.

— It turns either right or left.

— It has a wavy flight like that of larks (sometimes, in contrast, it falls like a stone: the paper is too heavy).

These three defects must be corrected.

Preventing the Wing from Leaning Sideways

To prevent the sideways lean, fold the wing exactly into two in the center (in particular, the fold must be in the middle of the glued part) so that, from the front, it resembles an open V.

As soon as the wing leans toward one side, air friction becomes stronger on that side and raises the wing (similar to the shuttlecock in badminton):

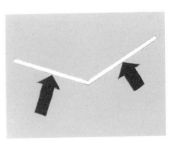

Wind forces

27

Preventing the Wing from Turning Randomly

The wing must be given some sort of vertical stabilizers or fins at the end of the wings by folding upward 1 centimeter (.4 inch) of each end (attention: the same amount on both sides!). These fins will play about the same role as the keel of a boat. As soon as the wing tends to glide a little sideways, the fins become sideways with

respect to the movement so that air friction puts them back into the correct direction.

Twisting the fins toward the right or the left corrects the wing's tendency to turn either right or left so that it flies straight. If this does not help, the wing is either twisted or badly folded or has two unequal "halves." It is not worth trying to repair it, make a new one.

Giving the Wing a Straight Flight

If a wing flies in a wavy manner like a lark, it does so because it is still trying to act like a dead leaf; in other words, its front is not heavy enough. A paper clip attached at the center of the front edge, or sometimes two clips at an equal distance from the center fold (see figure e, p. 27) adds enough weight. This provides the further advantage of flattening out the folds even more.

And now you must learn the knack of launching the wing. The ideal way is to throw the wing in the correct position and

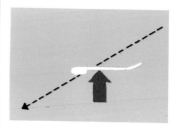

at the right speed, that is, a speed at which it flies straight.

If it is thrown too slowly, air friction is too weak to support it and the wing starts to fall. While falling, the speed increases, which helps the wing to straighten and to fly correctly afterward.

If the wing is thrown too fast, air friction is too strong and the

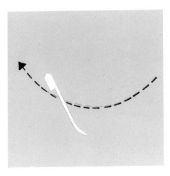

wing pulls upward.

While flying upward, the wing slows, of course, perhaps too much so that it starts to fall as if it had been thrown too

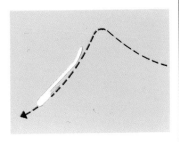

slowly.

If the wing is well thrown, it does not have a tendency to fall or to pull up.

Moreover, the expression "throwing" is not entirely correct: one should not throw it but it should be *released* at a correct speed.

How Can We Make a Wing Turn?

We have learned that by twisting the fins a little, it is possible to correct the wing's tendency to turn all by itself. To make it turn on purpose, the same method must be used. However, this is more difficult.

Indeed, for a wing to make a perfect turn, it must be tilted toward the inside of the curve. To do this it should be twisted so that one of the wings has more lift than the other. With some practice one can succeed, but it is certainly not very easy. This is one of the reasons that real gliders have not only wings but also a tail. We therefore abandon our flying wing to talk about more sophisticated models that are, however, more dif-

ficult to make: real gliders with tails.

What Is the Use of the Tail in a Glider?

The tail has several uses and, furthermore, several parts: a vertical fixed stabilizer or fin at the back of which is attached the rudder, which can turn either right or left (like that of a boat), and two small horizontal wings (stabilizers) the back part of which can turn upward or downward.

The vertical fin, like those of our flying wing, helps to maintain the glider in the same flight direction. The vertical rudder or, simply, rudder makes the glider turn right or left exactly as does the rudder of a boat, and

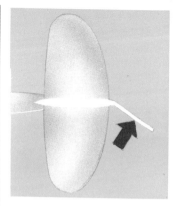

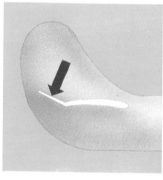

for the same reason.

And the small movable wings, called elevators, attached to the tail? They play the same role as the raised back edge (by means of the glued corner) of the flying wing: to lift the nose of the aircraft just enough. If the small wings are raised, air friction makes the tail of the glider go down so that the nose is lifted.

To be effective, these small wings need not be very large because they are far away from the center of the aircraft. To make something turn, for instance a merry-go-round in a public park, it is easier to push it far from the center.

The nose of a flying wing was raised by means of the upward curvature of its back edge: it did not need a tail. Why not keep the same system for real gliders? Well, because the wings of a glider must be curved in the other direction, down.

Why? Let us talk about this right now.

Glider

The Shape of the Wing

We have learned about what happens when a thin, smooth plate, such as a wooden board or a sheet of rigid paper, is moved in water or air. We shall talk from now on about real gliders, real planes, and birds. These are not thin plates that move in air but thick wings with a particular shape.

I n a cross section, a wing always has a shape of this kind:

The upper part (or top of the wing) is convex and the lower part (or bottom of the wing) is flat or even slightly concave. Why? The explanation is rather difficult, and we start with an experiment.

An Experiment

Take a sheet of paper, such as that for an ordinary typewriter, and hold it horizontally: it bends slightly downward.

Hold the sheet at the level of your mouth, and blow along its

upper surface: the sheet rises! If one stops blowing, it drops downward; if one blows again, it rises again.

At first sight, this is very astonishing: one would expect the sheet to bend more when blowing over it! Right? Why does it behave in such a strange way? Let us first see what happens when one does not blow and it lies there.

Air Pressure

Even though it is invisible, the air surrounding us presses against us, against the ground, and against all objects around us. *Careful*: do not confuse these *forces of pressure* with *air friction*. Friction occurs only when an object moves with respect to the air, whereas the unseen forces of pressure exist even when the air and the object are still.

For instance, air pressure makes orange juice rise in a straw. Indeed, air presses everywhere upon the surface of the juice except in the straw because there we suck up air. Therefore, air pressure makes juice in the glass rise in the straw.

Let us return to our sheet of paper. When we do not blow, air pressure is exerted equally on both sides of the sheet (otherwise it does not remain in place!): air pressure is the same on both sides.

When we blow along the upper surface, nothing changes underneath the sheet, but along the upper surface the air moves with a certain speed. Since the sheet rises, it means that the air above (the air that moves) is pressing less than the air underneath the sheet (which is still the way it was before).

Here we have an example of a general law demonstrated in physics that says that air that moves along a surface exerts less pressure upon this surface than if the air were still—and *increasingly less pressure with greater speed.*

The Difference Between the Top and the Bottom of a Wing

To study a wing, it is much easier to place it immobile inside a wind tunnel where air circulates at whatever speed we wish (we have already mentioned this in regard to the girl's hair on a bicycle).

Let us imagine a wing with a convex top and a concave bottom in a wind tunnel (in the picture below, the thin lines represent air currents that circulate in a wind tunnel).

At the bottom, which is flat, these lines are straight and parallel to each other (as if the wing were not there). However, along the top, because of the curvature, the lines come closer together before straightening out again. They come closer together because air has less room to move: since as much air flows here as elsewhere, it must naturally move faster along the top than anywhere else in the tunnel—in particular, faster than along the bottom of the wing.

It is possible to realize in another way that air moves faster on the convex side: to move from the leading edge to the trailing edge of the wing, air uses the same amount of time on both sides. However, on the convex side a kind of detour exists, meaning that a longer distance must be crossed. Therefore, air must move faster.

Hence, air moves faster along the top of the wing than along the bottom. And since it presses on the surface *increasingly less the faster it moves* along this surface, air presses less on the top

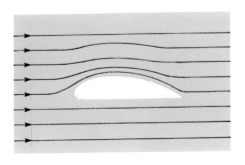

than on the bottom of the wing, which means that the wing is lifted.

Furthermore, the difference between air friction on the bottom and the top increases with the speed of air with respect to the wing: the faster the air, the more the wing is lifted.

And if the Wing Is Inclined?

If the wing is slightly inclined, the two effects are combined: that of the shape of the wing and that of its position. Because of its shape, air presses more upon the bottom than upon the top, and because of the inclination, air presses even more on the bottom, just as on a thin inclined plate.

However, if the inclination—called the angle of attack—is increased more and more, a critical angle is reached at which the effect of the shape decreases rapidly. If one observes the lines of air currents (there are several ways to do this in a wind tunnel), one finds that these lines have changed into turbulence along the upper surface of the wing.

It is clear that when the effect of the shape disappears, a wing is much less sustained: there is thus an angle of attack that should not be passed. We shall return to this problem in regard to landing of planes.

Lift and Drag

If the wing is not inclined at all with respect to the lines of air currents, it is sustained by the effect of its shape.

However, at the same time, it is pushed backward by the force with which air presses on its leading edge:

There are therefore two forces exerted by air upon the wing: a "good" one that lifts it (called *lift*) and a "bad" one that pulls the wing backward (called *drag*).

If we compare the wing to a thin plate, we notice that without inclination, the situation is very different:

The plate is not submitted to force, whereas the wing is both raised by the lift and pulled backward by the drag.

If the plate or the wing is slightly inclined, the effect of inclination is added: now the plate and the wing are both raised by the lift and pulled backward by the drag (see figure.)

Furthermore, the forces of the air are exerted not only on the wings but also on the body of the plane and on its tail. To study these forces, a larger wind tunnel is needed or a small-scale

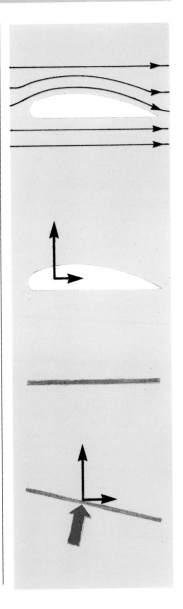

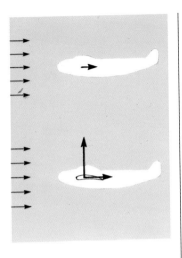

model of the plane. At any rate, one notices that air pushes the object backward with a force that depends heavily upon the shape of the plane. To prevent too much drag, the plane must have an *aerodynamic* shape (which more or less resembles that of a fish; as a matter of fact, not astonishing at all).

Finally, if one looks at the entire plane in a wind tunnel, one sees that air raises it (lift) and pulls it backward.

We have learned that the action of an air current at a certain speed on a motionless plane has the same effect as moving that plane at a certain speed in still air. When the plane flies, air friction produces both a lift (which sustains the plane in the air) and a drag (which brakes its movement). These two forces depend simultaneously upon the shape (the wings and the body) and the inclination of the wings with respect to the direction of movement.

We now find these two forces (the good one and the bad one) acting in the flight of gliders, planes, and birds.

But before takeoff, let us just briefly observe another effect of shape: the sailboat that is sailing to windward.

When we mentioned it earlier, we said that the curvature of the sail also had a role to play.

Indeed, what we have here is exactly a bulging "wing," which is very little inclined with respect to the direction of the wind.

Both for the sail and the wing, the curvature plays an important role, in particular when sailing with the smallest practical angle to the wind.

Gliders

How does a glider remain in the air? Some force is necessary to support it, to push it upward. This force is of course the lift. However, for this force to exist, the glider must have a certain speed. Without speed, no air friction, no lift, and hence . . . crash!

However, if lift exists, there must necessarily also be a drag that pulls the glider backward: its speed decreases! How is it capable of flying?

H ere is the sad situation of the pilot of a glider:

— His weight pulls him to the ground (let us imagine a heavy person asleep).

— He is sustained by a "good spirit" (the lift).

— But at the same time as the "good spirit" appears, *naturally* his brother, the "evil spirit" (the drag), hinders the glider and decreases its speed.

So that it does not fall, the glider must maintain its speed: it must find something or somebody that counteracts the evil spirit. On a regular plane, this is taken care of by the engine, but on a glider? Well, we shall have the lazy guy do something. No, we shall not wake him up! It is enough to incline the glider just a little bit forward so that the drag is overcome by the pull of the weight. If the inclination is just perfect, the action of the evil spirit is counterbalanced; everything goes well. However, the glider descends slowly through the air. *A glider can fly only by descending through the air.*

Gliding without noise through the air in a gli r is certainly the most pleasant way to play being a bird! Nevertheless, one must know how.

How Can a Glider Rise?

At first sight, this seems impossible. We have just learned that a glider flies only by descending slowly through the air.

And if a mass of rising air exists simultaneously? The glider finds itself in the situation of a fly that glides to the ground of an elevator while the elevator rises three floors. While descending through the air, the fly is lifted from the ground!

Similarly for a glider to be lifted from the ground *while descending through the air*, it must be in a rising air current, called an *ascending* air current, a situation that very much resembles that of the elevator and the fly.

There are several types of ascending air currents: for example to pass over a mountaintop, the wind must rise before descending again. There is therefore one slope of the mountaintop on which air rises, and by following this slope, a glider can be lifted.

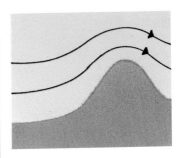

However, the most frequent and most useful ascending air currents form in places where air is warmer than elsewhere.

Hot air is lighter than cold air: this is the reason the smoke of a burning stick rises, hot air balloons rise, and it is warmer in the top gallery of a theater than in the parterre. Some areas in the countryside use solar heat better than others. Above a village or field of wheat, air is warmer than above a wooded area or a meadow. This hot air rises and can be used as an "elevator" by a glider.

The pilot of a glider must therefore be able to find such ascending air currents. He or she may of course look for fields of wheat, villages, and all other

While gliding to the floor of the elevator, the fly is lifted from the ground.

places where chances exist for warmer air. However, there are other means. For example, an ascending air current often generates a white puffy cloud called a cumulus: the pilot flies underneath this cumulus, which can be seen from far away, and glides in circles while being lifted by the air current. The same method is used, for the same reason, by another "pilot" of a glider, at the same time a glider itself—the vulture.

To be able to glide for a long time, one must know how to find and use ascending air currents.

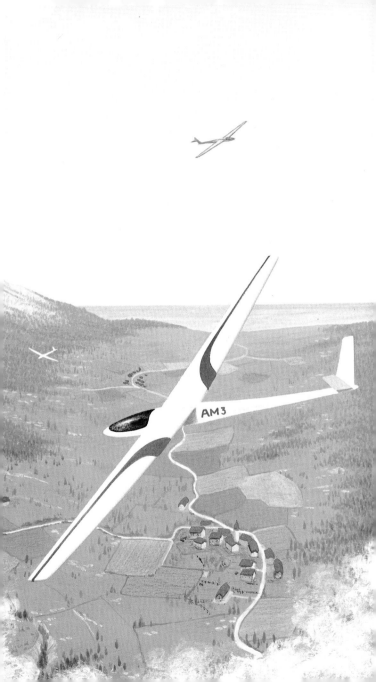

Circling in Air to Rise

Some people believe that vultures circle in the air because they are waiting for prey to fall upon. However, when a vulture has found something edible, it swoops down and devours it without waiting for another bird to steal it. So why does the vulture fly in circles? To rise.

A vulture is a very heavy bird. It cannot flap its wings for long without becoming exhausted because it is very hard work for the muscles. Vultures therefore spend much of their time gliding without moving their wings. However, when gliding, one descends slowly through the air. To rise, an ascending air current must be found. When the vulture has found one, it glides around in it in circles and hence rises slowly without any effort. When it has risen high enough, it flies straight and thus descends slowly for some miles until it has found another "elevator," another ascending air current where it rises again slowly, gliding in circles. This is

Flying vultures

how some vultures fly 200 kilometers (124 miles) in one day without moving their wings except during takeoff in the morning.

Vultures know how to use other kinds of ascending air currents, those that are formed by wind blowing over the crest of a hill. When the vulture finds a favorable crest, it follows it along in order to remain as long as possible in the ascending air current.

Many heavy birds do the same when they fly better than vultures. Storks, for instance, spend much time in gliding. However, they have a particular way of finding ascending air currents. They do not actually search for them, but since they usually fly in flocks, each bird keeping a certain distance from the other, sooner or later one of the storks is caught in an ascending air current. At that time, all the other storks join in and use the elevator together. Thereafter, they fly again in a V-shaped formation and continue their long voyage.

Flying Fish Do Not Fly

At least, they do not really fly: they glide.

However, to glide, one must have a certain speed: gliders do not take off by themselves. They are either towed by an aircraft and released only at a certain elevation, and at a certain speed, or a catapult hurls them at great speed from the top of a cliff, for example. What catapults flying fish? Usually

fear. But how?

They start by swimming at the surface of the water until they have reached enough speed that all of the upper part of the body is out of the water (similar to water skis or speedboats). At that point, the fish functions like a hydrofoil while its tail (its engine) is still in the water. It then moves its tail very fast, and because its body is no longer hindered by water resistance since it has emerged, its

How to Bank the Glider in a Sharp Turn

To take a turn with a bicycle, one must lean toward the inside. By the way, this is done automatically: one has a feeling for the correct inclination, which depends upon speed.

To provide cars, too, with such an inclination, the outer side of highways is raised along curves. Otherwise, cars would tend to drive straight ahead and hence skid.

Well, a glider also "skids" if it is turned without banking by turning only the rudder. The glider therefore starts to move sideways like a crab, it loses speed, and descends. To bank a glider correctly, it must be inclined toward the center of the curve. How is this done?

Talking about the flying wing, we mentioned earlier that turning was possible by twisting the wings a bit so that the one facing the inside of the curve is a little more raised on its trailing edge. However, this was a critical procedure, and the flying wing was damaged. Nevertheless, this procedure was used for the first gliders before 1900, but soon something bet-

speed becomes very great. It then opens its large fins, which play the role of wings, and—it takes off. However, as soon as the fish has left the water, its "engine" does not work anymore and it thus glides in the air some tens of meters before falling back into the water. Perhaps the tunafish that wanted to swallow it has given up when it saw the fish disappear? If not, all the flying fish can do is to start all over again!

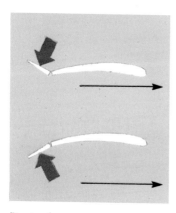

Direction of movement

ter was invented: ailerons.

Each wing of a glider has on its trailing edge a small movable part that can be raised or lowered: this is the *aileron*.

When an aileron is raised, air friction presses upon it downward: the wing is pushed down. In contrast, when the aileron is lowered, air friction pushes it upward and the wing lifts.

The controls of the two ailerons are not independent: when the left one is lowered, the right one is lifted by the same amount. Planes sometimes test their ailerons before takeoff: one is lifted while the other is lowered like the flippers of a swimmer doing the crawl.

What controls the ailerons is the control stick that the pilot holds vertically between the legs. If the pilot turns it to the left, the left aileron rises and the right aileron lowers and the plane banks toward the left side. It "follows" the control shift.

At the same time, the pilot swings the rudder in the good direction by pushing his or her feet on a horizontal bar called the *rudder bar*. If the pilot pushes with the left foot, the rudder swings toward the left and the glider turns left.

Therefore, to turn left, one must at the same time turn the control stick to the left side and push with the left foot on the rudder bar—just the right amount! If the glider is not banked enough, it skids to the right and loses speed. If it is banked too much, the glider sideslips toward the center of the curve on the left and loses altitude. Of course, all this is very tricky. However, our senses help us to find the right combination (just as on the bicycle): if banking puts the pilot straight upward on the seat, he did the right thing.

And the elevators (the small horizontal, movable wings on the tail that allow the raising or lowering of the glider's nose)? How are these operated? Also

If the pilot pulls the controls stick toward him, the glider raises its nose.

with the control stick, however this time by pushing it forward (the elevators turn downward and the aircraft lowers its nose) or pulling it backward (the aircraft lifts its nose).

In short, the control stick commands both the ailerons (if it is turned left or right) and the elevators (if it is pushed forward or pulled backward). The rudder bar, on the other hand, controls the rudder.

These are the controls of a glider and they are also the major controls of a plane. One more thing to do with a plane is to control the power of the engine. This is what we are going to learn now.

Planes

A plane has only one more device than a glider, but a very important one: an engine. This time, to the list for the unhappy pilot of a glider should be added another spirit that pulls forward and counterbalances the drag: it is no longer necessary to incline the aircraft forward to use the pull of weight. A plane can fly horizontally without searching for ascending currents.

A plane can also rise and even take off by itself, whereas a glider must be towed into the air or launched from the top of a cliff with a catapult.

Takeoff

This is the most exciting moment for the traveler; in fact, we are still not used to losing contact with the ground and seeing the countryside tip over and become smaller.

For the pilot, this is a critical moment.

First, the engine must be well heated and everything must be under control because this is the time when it is required to make its greatest effort. Therefore, having reached the beginning of the takeoff runway, the plane stops and its engines are pushed at full throttle while it stands still.

Furthermore, the pilot must be aware of the direction of the wind. The best way to take off is against the wind. Indeed, what keeps the plane in the air as soon as it has lifted from the ground is a force that depends upon the speed of the plane *with respect to the air*. For the same ground speed, the speed with respect to the air is greater if facing the wind. In the same way, we know which way to run to launch a kite in a small breeze.

This is also known by birds, at least heavy birds, which must run to gain speed before taking off. It is said that the brothers

Lilienthal, by their observation of the takeoff of storks against the wind, brought to aviation one of its first breakthroughs at the end of the nineteenth century.

Therefore, one always chooses the end of a runway that allows the plane to take off most closely against the wind. Large airports have many runways in the shape of a cross or even a star so that this kind of takeoff is always possible.

Here we have the plane at the end of the runway, facing the wind, with a hot engine. It starts to roll, accelerating very fast. From this moment on, things change according to whether the plane has a propeller engine or a jet engine.

A propeller airplane usually has its tail in a low position at rest. To gain speed when running, it must "erase" the wings and place itself in a horizontal position. Therefore, its tail must be lifted, and by activating the elevators, the pilot pushes

the control stick forward, but not too much.

A jet airplane usually has its body in a horizontal position at rest (its third wheel is underneath its nose). A jet airplane accelerates in this position.

When the necessary speed is reached, the pilot pulls the control stick toward him in order to lower the tail of the plane and place the wings more fully against the wind. The plane takes off.

Here, too, the difference between the propeller and the jet airplane is great.

A jet airplane has a large supply of power. It retracts its wheels (this greatly decreases the drag) and accelerates at top speed, climbing very rapidly.

A propeller airplane, as soon as it has lifted from the ground, retracts its wheels (for the same reason), but it shifts into a horizontal position

A jet airplane is much more powerful than a propeller airplane and can therefore take off more steeply.

again, or almost, in order to accelerate more before climbing. Indeed, its power supply is much smaller and if it tried to climb as steeply as a jet, it would lose speed and stall just as a glider launched upward. It is not the time for a propeller airplane to do that just a few meters off the ground! It must gain much speed before climbing appreciably—and even then, a propeller plane cannot climb very fast.

At a certain elevation, and at high speed, one notices that the plane "decreases the size of its wings"; that is, it retracts its flaps, which were extended until now. Why?

The force that supports a plane (the lift) depends upon the speed, the position of the wings, and also their surface. At low speed, this surface must be larger. This is why modern planes have flaps that enlarge the trailing edge, flaps that are extended during takeoff and landing (see diagram).

However, as soon as a certain speed is reached, these flaps are retracted. It is true that lift would increase if the flaps were not retracted, but this would not be of any help because drag would also increase, requiring much more fuel. This is why planes fly very high.

Why Fly Very High?

Because with the same consumption of fuel, one flies faster. Indeed, the higher the

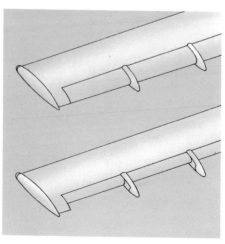

It is more pleasant to fly above atmospheric turbulence.

plane, the lighter the air. Because of its weight, air tends to become denser close to the ground than at high altitude. At 10,000 meters (32,810 feet), air is lighter than at 2000 meters (6510 feet).

With decreasing density of the air, air friction toward a moving body also decreases: in a lighter air, air friction, at the same speed, is thus lower. In other words, the same air friction is obtained with greater speed.

To remain airborne, a plane must therefore fly faster at 10,000 meters (32,810 feet) altitude than at 2000 (6510 feet). And since both the "good spirit" and the "evil spirit" are the same, even though the plane flies faster at 10,000 meters (32,810 feet), it is not braked more by the air than at 2000 meters (6510 feet), and hence the engine does not have to be more powerful.

Therefore, using the same amount of fuel, the plane flies

much farther in 1 hour at 10,000 meters (32,810 feet) than at 2000 (6510 feet). It is more pleasant for passengers who do not like to remain seated for too many hours, and it is less expensive for airlines. Another advantage for passengers is that air turbulence is much less violent at high altitude. Finally, everybody is happy that planes fly very high because they are heard less—unless one is unlucky enough to live close to an airport.

Thus our plane at high altitude rapidly approaches its destination. It must now land.

Landing

"Fasten your seat belts, we are beginning our descent"—a descent that will last about half an hour. Indeed, the plane not only must descend but must also slow its speed: a plane that flies normally at 900 kilometers/hour (560 miles/hour) lands at less than 300 kilometers/hour (185 miles/hour).

It must therefore be at the right place, at the right elevation, and at the right speed. If everything goes well and if the landing strip is cleared, the pilot receives permission to land,

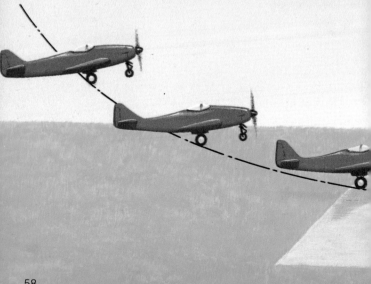

that is, to decrease the remainder of both its elevation and speed.

This is another critical moment for the pilot—a little less than at takeoff because the plane is lighter: after having crossed the Atlantic, it carries some 20 tons less fuel. It can thus be sustained by the air when slowing its speed, which helps during landing.

A perfect landing is a soft one when the plane lands without bumping against the ground and bouncing back after having touched it a first time. Therefore, after having decreased speed as much as possible, it is necessary to level off in order to land horizontally.

How can it be landed slowly?

At first, both in order to brake the plane and keep it airborne, even when its speed is much lower, its nose must be lifted. Thereafter, for the same reasons, it must land facing the wind. Thus the plane descends and its speed decreases. However, this decrease in speed must be carefully calculated: if the speed is too high when the plane touches the ground, it runs the risk of smashing its wheels or reaching the end of the runway before having come to a complete stop.

If, on the other hand, the plane is still in the air with a speed that has become too low to remain airborne, it falls.

Let us suppose that the pilot has calculated well but that he

comes close to the ground at a time when the plane's speed has become too low. How can he do the leveling off glide before contact? He must straighten the plane, namely, raise its tail and accelerate to gain enough speed just before touching the ground.

Of course, during the descent, the pilot has extended the flaps that enlarge the wings. He may thus remain airborne at lower speeds.

Moreover, there is another device that one can sometimes observe functioning if one is seated above the wing. A few minutes before landing, one can see the leading edge of the wing separate slightly, leaving between that part and the rest of the wing a slot, called the leading edge slot. What is the function of that slot?

In the last stage of landing, the wing is quite inclined with respect to the direction movement. There is thus a risk that small air streams separate from the top of the wing, creating turbulence that in turn prevents the shape (the airfoil) from acting to support the plane. Well, the leading edge slot prevents such air streams from separating, or at least it allows the wing to be inclined much more than if the slot were not there. Why? This again is too difficult to explain in a few words. But it works well.

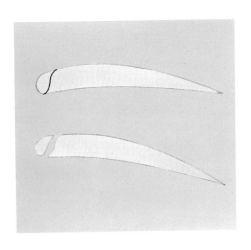

Birds

They have been flying much longer than humans. In a book entitled How Things Fly *it is impossible not to ask oneself how the real specialists in flight do it!*

Well, the way birds learned how to fly has evolved through millions of years. We can shorten their history to 10 minutes—on paper. In fact, we know enough about the techniques of flying to "invent a bird!"

How can a warm blooded animal with a skeleton become capable of flying?

To Invent a Bird

First, let us not talk about large birds (we shall soon see why). Let us simply invent a rather small bird, about the size of a blackbird.

To start with, it needs wings that are both strong and light. If we can come up with a really brilliant idea, we shall invent the feather. We shall soon see why this is such a brilliant idea.

Furthermore, our bird must be light.

Let's start by giving it empty bones: these are lighter than full bones and have the same strength. This is why the frame of a bicycle is made of tubes.

The bird will not make great use of legs: let's make them thin and light. No fat! The bird will not be able to store food: it will have to eat often. In order that its food does not make it too heavy, let us choose nourishing substances (grains and insects) and provide rapid digestion. Finally, it is better for birds to lay eggs instead of carrying their

Flying ducks

offspring in their bellies until delivery!

After lightness comes the shape: it must be streamlined to decrease air friction. Legs must be retractable during flight like wheels of a plane. All muscles must be grouped together toward the center of the body. The head must be small and light: heavy jaws and muscles to activate them must be omitted.

All muscles of the bird are grouped together in the middle of the body. This picture shows flying storks.

A light beak will serve to catch foods that will be crushed inside the stomach by the gizzard.

So much for its structure. How about the engine? To fly requires hard work. Powerful muscles are needed to move the wings, in particular to pull them down since this movement makes the bird rise. These very strong muscles cover the chest (the white meat of the

The breastbone, *a very solid attachment for the muscles that move the wings.*

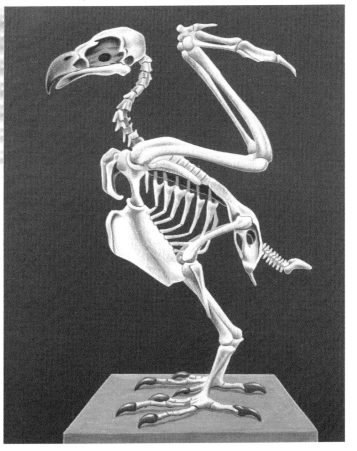

chicken), and since they need a very solid attachment the farthest possible away from the center of the body, the skeleton of birds consists in front of a special bony crest, the breastbone.

These powerful muscles must be fed. A bird must have a rapid blood circulation, a rather large heart, and an efficient digestive system. Moreover, it must eat a lot! " To eat like a bird" is sometimes used for people who eat very little. However, this expression is certainly not very well chosen! Birds eat a lot of food for their size. In fact, they have a ferocious appetite!

Therefore, a lot of perfecting is needed to produce a bird. The most extraordinary device is certainly the feather.

Why Do Birds Have Feathers?

First of all, like all mammals, birds must be covered with "clothes" so that their bodies keep a constant temperature, day and night, summer and winter. The feathers of a bird thus play the same role as the fur of mammals, with one further advantage: lightness. Their

down is both very warm and very light.

However, feathers play the greatest role for the wings and the tail. In fact, they are "dead." Once they have grown, the body no longer feeds them and this permits the wings to be very light. Without feathers, the wings would have to be covered by a membrane with blood vessels to nourish it, to protect it, and so on. Because of feathers, all this extra burden is not necessary.

Although they are very light, feathers provide a very strong surface that repairs itself if damaged! This is easy to observe: if one "tears" a feather a little bit, smoothing it between your fingers is enough to erase the "tear." A feather is made of barbs that interlock by means of small hooks. If two barbs have been separated, it is enough to put them close together again. The hooks join and the feather is like new!

Finally, the feathers of wings

have a marvelous characteristic: they can rotate like the slats of a venetian blind. When the wing is lowered to press on the air, the feathers are all flattened out. A wing looks like a single sheet.

However, when the wing rises to decrease air friction,

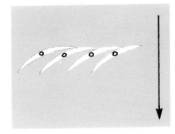

which is then in the wrong direction, the feathers rotate and provide a smaller surface to the air:

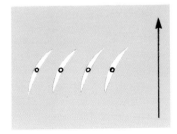

We have to admit that we could not have done better.

67

How Do Birds Fly?

What sustains a plane in the air is air friction on its wings, which do not move, a friction produced by the movement of the plane by means of its engine. The situation of the bird is quite different: with its wings, a bird must both sustain itself and move. In other words, these wings simultaneously play the role of the wings of a plane and that of its propeller.

The various species of birds offer a great variety of solutions to this problem.

A pigeon's entire wing takes part in flapping and describes a kind of inclined figure eight.

Half the time, the wing low-

ers as it goes forward. It is widely spread out, and its large feathers are well flattened so that the wing exposes the largest possible surface. Air friction is very great and directed upward: it supports the pigeon well, but it is also directed backward so that it brakes the bird.

Thereafter, the wing goes backward. It is a little bit flexed, its feathers rotate to let through some air, and, above all, the position of the wing is changed: it is almost vertical so that air friction is almost horizontal: air no longer brakes the bird but pushes it forward.

When the half-flexed wing arrives at the top and at the

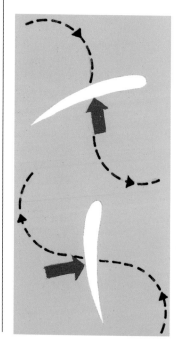

back, the wing spreads out again, its large feathers flatten out, and the downstroke of the wing starts again. Therefore, during one flapping of the wing, there is a moment of lift and a moment of forward movement. If these movements are quite rapid, the bird flies straight ahead on a regular course. Otherwise, it flies as seen in the picture below.

These different movements are found partly in other species, but important variations exist. For instance, the part of a duck's wing that is closest to the body does not move much: it remains more or less in the position of a plane's wing. It is only the external half of the wing that flaps and provides a forward movement to the bird.

Other birds fly in an interme-

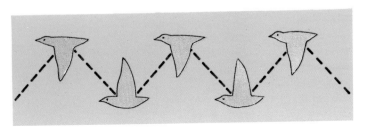

diary fashion between that of a pigeon and that of a duck, including the seagull when it does not glide through gusty winds along the seashore.

Below are represented the various flying techniques in a front view:

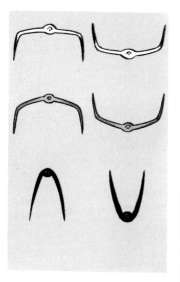

Of course, there are many more species of birds with their own particular ways of flying. The most extraordinary one is perhaps the family of humming-birds (in French, *oiseaux-mouches*). Their name in French derives from their tiny size (that of a fly [*mouche*]) and

in English from the sound of their rapidly moving wings. These move so fast that they become invisible! Humming-birds are capable of hovering in place—without wind—while with their long tongue they extract the nectar of a flower.

To do this, they keep their bodies in a vertical position and beat their wings forward and backward, often as many as 50 times per second. Their wings are capable of bending in both directions.

Air friction changes from forward to backward so that the bird does not move, but air pushes just a little upward, too, and sustains the tiny weight of the bird.

Hummingbirds are also capable of flying very fast (one cannot follow them with our eyes) and also of crossing thousands of kilometers during their migrations!

The Landing of Birds

Birds must descend and slow down. However, instead of doing the two things together as planes do, they slow down only at the last second.

They start by descending while folding their wings a little. Thus, they are less supported so that they dive toward the ground while their speed increases. At the very last moment, they brake by opening their wings widely, thus forming a sort of plane perpendicular to the direction of movement:

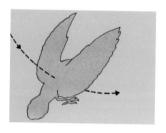

ported so that they dive toward the ground while their speed increases. At the very last moment, they brake by opening their wings widely, thus forming a sort of plane perpendicular to the direction of movement:

However, like planes, they level off at the very last second, and for the same reason: to protect their "landing gear," namely their legs in the case of birds that land on the ground or on a branch. Those that land on water touch the surface of the water first with the chest, which is well protected with its rounded cushion of muscles, rather than with the legs or belly. Whoever has done a belly landing when diving in water understands this precaution very well.

Birds at Takeoff

The method used depends a lot upon the species. Small birds, such as sparrows, start by flexing their legs and then they jump into the air, extending them all of a sudden. It is only in the air that they start flapping their

wings, making a figure eight, as in regular flight. However, this time, the figure eight is horizontal since movements are made to rise (which demands a great effort). This is how small birds are able to take off vertically.

Heavier birds must take off obliquely like planes. They gain speed by running against the wind (if there is any wind) with their wings spread out. This is how pheasants and vultures take off. Wading birds do the same with an extra advantage: the length of their legs allows them to flap their wings while running.

As to "hydroplanes," that is, heavy birds taking off in water, such as ducks, swans, and pelicans, they start by beating the water strongly with their legs so that the front of their bodies is raised above the water—just like a speedboat. Thus freed from water friction, they continue to swim faster and faster, flapping their wings until they have gained enough speed to take off.

Finally some, species—many birds of prey, for instance—choose for their nests a high overhanging place from which the bird can dive while gliding to gain speed without flapping its wings.

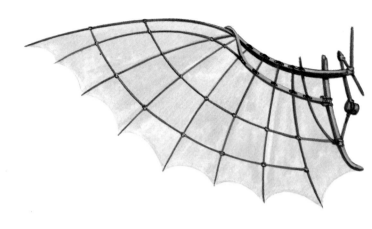

Can Humans Fly?

Of course we mean *really* fly—not glide—without an engine!

This is certainly a very ancient dream and many trials have been made. Leonardo da Vinci, for example, designed several contraptions called ornithopters at the end of the fifteenth century that should have allowed people to fly. He studied birds very carefully, and most of his ornithopters resembled large skeletons of birds with wings made with a fabric that humans were supposed to move. But none of these inventions worked for one reason: although birdlike structures were copied (including feathers, beak, and empty bones), a bird the size of a human being could absolutely not fly!

Let us imagine, for instance, a sparrow the size of a human being. It would have wings measuring 2 square meters (2.4 square yards) and would weigh about a hundred kilograms (220 pounds). However, with wings that size, the heaviest living bird, the condor, is barely able to fly. It weighs, however, only 15 kilograms (33 pounds)! A bird weighing 100 kilograms (220 pounds) would need wings measuring at least 20 square meters (24 square yards). To move such wings, more than

100 kilograms (220 pounds) of muscles would be required!

Indeed, if we multiply by 3 the size of a bird, for example, the surface of its wings is multiplied by 9 (3 x 3), but its weight is multiplied by 27 (3 x 3 x 3)!

This is the reason large birds (predators or marine birds) do not have the plump shape of a sparrow: they have wings that are much longer with respect to their bodies. Remember that we called the condor "the largest bird." This is not correct: an ostrich, for example, is much larger. However, it does not fly!

So, humans cannot fly? This was true until only a few years ago when a man succeeded in crossing the English Channel, at an elevation of a few meters, on a very light hang glider fitted with a large propeller that was moved with pedals. This was the best that modern materials and techniques could offer, and the man himself was a thin athlete with an exceptional muscular power for his weight.

In short, with this exception, humans cannot fly!

This hang glider, called the Gossamer Albatross, crossed the English Channel in 1979.

Index

Numbers in italics refer to illustrations.

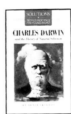

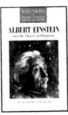

BARRON'S
FOCUS ON SCIENCE Series

This pocket-sized series explores each topic, with exciting texts and lots of sparkling full-color illustrations. (Age 13 & up). Each book: Paperback, index & bibliography, approx. 80 pp., 4¼″ × 7⅛″, $4.95, Can. $6.95. Each book: contains a handy index and bibliography.

Titles include:

THE ATMOSPHERE, *Maury,* ISBN 4213-1

THE ATOM, *Averous,* ISBN 3837-1

BIOLOGY'S BUILDING BLOCKS, *Chevallier-Le Guyader,* ISBN 4212-3

CLIMATES: PAST, PRESENT AND FUTURE, *Tordjman,* ISBN 3838-X

DESTINATION: OUTER SPACE, *Alter,* ISBN 3839-8

DINOSAURS AND OTHER EXTINCT ANIMALS, *Beaufay,* ISBN 3836-3

EARTH AND THE CONQUEST OF SPACE, *Kohler,* ISBN 3831-2

HEAT AND COLD, *Maury,* ISBN 4211-5

HOW THINGS FLY, *Balibar & Maury,* ISBN 4215-8

LIFE AND DEATH OF DINOSAURS, *Chenel,* ISBN 3840-1

THE ORIGIN OF LIFE, *Hagene & Lenay,* ISBN 3841-X

PREHISTORY, *Barloy,* ISBN 3835-5

VOLCANOES, *Kohler,* ISBN 3832-0

WEATHER, *Kohler,* ISBN 3833-9

All prices are in U.S. and Canadian dollars and subject to change without notice. Order from your bookstore, or direct from Barron's by adding 10% for postage & handling (minimum charge $1.50, Canada $2.00). N.Y. residents add sales tax. ISBN prefix: 0-8120

Barron's Educational Series, Inc.
250 Wireless Blvd. • Hauppauge, N.Y. 11788
Call toll-free: 1-800-645-3476, in N.Y.: 1-800-257-5729
In Canada: Georgetown Book Warehouse
34 Armstrong Ave. • Georgetown, Ont. L7G 4R9
Call toll-free: 1-800-668-4336